Contents

A Secret Wish

Fairy Pixie sat by the river, watching the bullfrogs hopping from one lily pad to another. She was feeling rather sorry for herself. There was to be a midsummer's night party in the fairy glade and no-one had invited her.

Pixie sighed and started making a daisy chain with pink-tipped daisies. But that didn't make her feel any better.

A sudden noise in the bushes behind made her look around. It was Fairy Midge picking fuchsia flowers. Pixie called out to her.

'Oh, hello, Pixie,' said Midge. 'Sorry, I can't stop. I have to dress all the fairies' hair for the party tonight! Do you think these fuchsia flowers will make a pretty head-dress?'

Fairy Pixie nodded wistfully, as Fairy Midge flew away, her arms full of the beautiful red and purple blossoms. She wished that she could be wearing such lovely flowers in her hair, but she wasn't even invited to the party, so there was no point in even thinking about it.

Pixie turned back to the bull-frogs, but they were too busy with their own hopping game to even notice her. She felt a single tear trickle down her cheek and drip off the end of her nose into the stream.

'There's no use in sitting here crying,' she scolded herself. 'I'll just go for a nice little walk.'

She wandered through the woods until she found herself by the enchanted wishing well. Pixie peered down into the deep darkness of the well.

'I wonder..?' she thought.

Suddenly, she made her mind up and closed her eyes and crossed her wing-tips.

'I wish,' she whispered, 'that I could go to the midsummer's night party tonight and that something very special would happen!'

There was a sudden whirr of flapping fairy-wings and Pixie found herself surrounded by all her fairy friends.

'Pixie!' said Fairy Polly. 'Why aren't you getting ready for the party tonight? You know you must be there... as special guest of honour!'

'Oh!' gasped Pixie, blushing with joy. 'Must I?'

'Of course you must!' interrupted Fairy Tina. 'You can't have forgotten, Pixie?'

'Forgotten what?' wondered Pixie. 'What was I supposed to remember?'

Fairy Polly just laughed and touched Pixie lightly on the head with her long sparkly wand.

'Silly Fairy!' she said. 'You were chosen to be this year's Fairy Queen, of course! Now, hurry and get ready! The party will be starting soon and Midge will be wondering where you are! She has some beautiful ivory magnolias to dress your hair with!'

Fairy Pixie couldn't believe it! Had she forgotten or had the wishing well just granted her secret wish? Now she would never know!

Party Purse PUZZLE

Polly Pocket loves her new Party Purse! But she's put some rather unusual things inside it! Can you guess which things Polly should not be carrying in her purse? The answers are at the bottom of the page.

These items don't belong in Polly's Party Purse: egg cup, teapot, ice-skates, goldfish.

POLLY'S NAUGHTY KITTENS

Oh dear! Polly went shopping and just look at the mess her naughty kittens made while she was out! It'll take her ages to tidy it up! Can you help? Draw in the missing items onto the second picture and then colour in the scene.

What's Wrong With The SCHOOL BELL?

It was Polly's first day as teacher at the brand new village school. She drove up in her car, parked behind the bicycle shed and walked into the playground. She looked to see if anyone was watching, then ran up the side steps and zoomed down the other side!

Polly looked in through the music room window at the piano. 'I hope the children like music lessons,' she thought. 'We shall have one music lesson every day!'

The next room she came to was the gymnasium. There were mats on the floor and a long mirror down one wall. 'We will be able to have dancing lessons in here as well as keeping fit,' Polly decided, looking at her watch.

She hurried inside the school, stopping to make sure that the drinks machine in the hall was working properly.

'I think I'll just have a cup of hot chocolate before the children arrive,' she said, putting her money in the slot. But she had pressed the wrong button and the machine made a frothy coffee instead!

Polly drank her delicious coffee as she hurried round all the newly painted classrooms. She made sure that the lights were all working and that every room had plenty of books, pens, pencils and paper.

Soon, it was almost time for school to begin.

Polly checked the time and went to ring the school bell. She pulled the bell rope, but nothing happened. She pulled it again, harder this time, but still nothing happened.

'What can be wrong?' Polly wondered, going outside to look up at the bell tower on the roof. She could just see it from the ground and the bell looked alright. It didn't look broken.

'Good morning, Miss Polly!' said Midge, arriving for lessons. 'I didn't hear the school bell ring!'

'I know,' said Polly. 'I don't know what's wrong with it!'

'What's wrong with what?' asked Tina, arriving with Lulu and Pixie. 'Good morning, Miss Polly!'

'The school bell doesn't seem to be working,' said Polly. 'I'll have to get someone to come and have a look at it.'

Just then Diddy and Wee Willie flew over the school in Diddy's stunt plane, making everyone jump.

'Hello, everyone!' yelled Diddy, waving to them. 'We thought we'd arrive in style for our first day at our new school!'

'What a clever idea!' said Polly, hurrying over to where the boys were landing in the school playground. She explained about the bell. Diddy got straight back into the stunt plane and flew up to the bell tower to take a closer look.

Everyone watched and waited as his plane circled the bell tower. Then he flew back to the playground.

'A bird has made its nest in the bell,' he explained.

'That's why it won't ring. There are four little chicks in the nest, you shouldn't move it, Miss Polly.'

'Of course not!' agreed Polly at once. 'But what am I to do about the bell until the birds are ready to leave their nest?'

'I know!' shouted Midge. 'I've got just the thing!' She reached deep into her school-bag and pulled out a referee's whistle. Then she put the whistle between her lips and blew hard!

'PHHHHEEEEEE-EEEEEP!'

Everyone covered their ears! Midge smiled and handed the whistle to Polly.

'Thank you, Midge!' said Polly. 'This whistle will make a perfect substitute for the school bell until the baby birds are old enough to leave home! Now, who's ready for school?'

Polly's Birthday Surprise

Lulu and Tina were working hard in the kitchen, getting the food ready for Polly's birthday party.

'Do you think we'll have enough jelly for the trifle, Lulu?' asked Tina, stirring a huge bowl of thick yellow custard.

'I hope so,' replied Lulu, pouring flour into a measuring bowl and covering her glasses with a film of white powder. 'I bought lots of jelly… Tina! You've been eating the cubes haven't you?'

Tina looked guilty. 'I didn't mean to eat so many of them,' she confessed. 'But they taste so delicious, like fruit gums!'

Just then, Fifi staggered into the kitchen with a huge crate which she set down in a corner.

'Oh la la' she gasped, staggering to a chair and collapsing on it. 'Je suis très fatigué!'

'Hello, Fifi,' said Tina, hiding a smile at the state of Fifi's dress.

It was all crumpled and covered in paw-prints! Lulu wiped the flour off her glasses and stared at Fifi. She couldn't believe her eyes! Their french friend always looked so chic and tidy, but today she looked as if she'd been wrestling with her two naughty poodles!

'I have come,' announced Fifi, when she got her breath back, 'to bake ze special cake for Polly's birthday!'

'Oh, goody!' said Lulu. 'I'm not having much luck with my cake recipe!'

Fifi set to work. Lulu and Tina watched as she whizzed round the kitchen, sifting flour, whisking eggs, making icing and proving what a great cook she was. Now and again the girls would glance curiously at the crate Fifi had brought with her. It made funny noises and seemed to move by itself!

'I wonder what's in the crate?' Lulu whispered, but Tina wasn't listening. She was running her fingers round one of Fifi's mixing bowls and licking the delicious mixture off her fingertips!

Soon the enormous cake was in the oven and the girls went off to get ready for Polly's party. Fifi carefully opened up the huge crate and reached inside for something.

That evening, when Polly's

party was in full swing, Fifi asked Lulu to help her carry the cake in from the kitchen.

'Voila!' she cried. 'Happy birthday, Polly, ma chèrie!'

'Oh, thank you, Fifi!' gasped Polly. 'What an enormous cake! Even Tina couldn't manage to eat that one all by herself. And so many candles!'

'Bet you can't blow them all out, Polly!' said Tina.

Polly took a deep breath and blew really hard. The candles

flickered and died. As they did so, Fifi took the top off the cake and out popped... two adorable tiny puppies!

'Oh, Fifi! They're beautiful!' laughed Polly, 'What a wonderful birthday surprise!'

Wildlife Park

The river is the one place used by all the animals in Polly's Wildlife Park. Every day, at sunset, they gather for a bath and a long cool drink. Look carefully and see if you can count how many animals there are in the picture. But watch out! Some may be hiding from you! Then try to guess their names. You can see if you were right by looking at the answers at the bottom of the page.

Answers: There are 17 animals. A leopard, zebra, giraffe, monkey, sloth, snake, lizard, lioness, 3 frogs, kingfisher, crocodile, 2 hippos and 2 elephants. Did you spot them all?

The Fairylight Ball

Fairy Tina was getting very impatient! She'd been waiting for Fairy Pixie and Fairy Midge for ages... and they still weren't ready for the Fairylight Ball! Tina frowned and blew on a dandelion clock to tell the time. It was nearly eight o'clock.

'Come on, you two!' she called, going behind a toadstool into the secret cave at the back of the Fairy Glade. 'It will be dark by the time we get to the ball if you don't hurry up. The other fairies will have eaten all the food... and I'm hungry!'

'You're always hungry!' laughed Pixie, twirling around in front of her mirror to get a better look at her new ballgown. 'How do you like my new earrings?'

'They're just great!' sighed poor Tina. 'Now please hurry up!'

'What's all the rush?' asked Fairy Midge, popping her head out of her toadstool dressing room. 'I have to feed the squirrels before we go, Tina. Do me a big favour and collect some nuts from the tree down by the river, will you?'

Tina went off to fetch the nuts, stamping her feet in their

dainty fairy slippers and scowling. Pixie and Midge watched her go, giggling.

'Well done, Midge!' chuckled Pixie. 'I'd never have been able to get ready with Tina making such a fuss!'

'I know,' smiled Midge. 'But she's right, you know. We are very late.'

'I only need to put on my pendant and brush my hair...'

'And feed the squirrels!' Pixie reminded her.

'And then I'll be ready!' agreed Midge.

At long last, they set off for the Ball. Darkness was falling and Tina was first to spot the Ballroom Fairylights glowing in the distance through the trees.

'Look! Look!' she pointed excitedly. 'I can see the Ballroom and the Funfair from here! There they are!'

As they drew nearer, the three

friends could see that the Ball was in full swing! Fairies were dancing, whirling round and round on the dance floor! They wore beautiful fairy ballgowns, encrusted with sparkling sequins and jewels, each one more dazzling and more magical than the last!

'I can't see Fairy Polly anywhere,' said Tina, looking around for her. 'Where can she be?'

'I don't know,' said Pixie, 'but I know where I'm going! Are you two coming?'

And she gathered up her petticoats and ran towards the Fairy Wheel! Tina and Midge weren't far behind her!

'This is wonderful!' yelled Tina, hanging out of the carriage, as the wheel carried them up and around, over and over again. 'Let's go round just one more time!'

'Ooh! My head is beginning to spin' reported Midge, 'And now I can see more stars than ever!'

After what seemed like the hundredth ride, the fairy friends climbed down, their legs a little wobbly, and looked around at all the other fairies having a wonderful time. There were fairies dancing, fairies singing, fairies running up and down the fabulous ballroom stairs… fairies everywhere! But still no sign of Fairy Polly.

Suddenly, someone started to shout. Pixie looked around to see who it was and saw that all the fairies were running out of the Ballroom into the Funfair! She and Tina and Midge decided to go outside too and see what was happening.

All the fairies were gathered round in a huge circle, cheering and clapping and looking up at a huge pink and golden striped hot-air balloon drifting down from the sky!

'How lovely!' gasped Pixie. 'It must be a very important guest arriving in such grand style!'

'I think you're right!' chuckled Tina, as she caught a glimpse of the person waving down from the balloon. It was someone very familiar, with golden hair and a happy smile! 'Fairy Polly!' shouted Pixie and Midge together. 'She's here! Hurrah!'

Fairy Polly stepped out of the

balloon basket as it touched the ground. She bowed to her guests and held up her fairy wand for silence. The cheers quietened down.

'Welcome, fairy friends, to my Fairylight Ball,' she smiled, looking round at the crowds. 'I hope you will all enjoy yourselves and have a wonderful time! Now, back to the dancing!'

Tina looked around at the fairytale scene. 'We will have a wonderful time,' she thought to herself, 'now that Fairy Polly is here at last!'

Fairy Midge and Fairy Pixie are down in the Fairy Glade, gathering flowers for the Fairy Midsummer's Ball! But they don't know that someone else is in the Glade too! Join the dots from 1 to 90 and see who it can be! Then colour the picture with your brightest colours. Have fun!
Who's In The Fairy Glade?
Answer: It's Fairy Polly! Were you right?

WONDERFUL WATER WORLD!

Polly and the gang love to spen day at Water World! It's one of their favourite places! Have a cl look at these two pictures. The look the same, but the bottom has 6 differences. See if you car find them all! The answers are the bottom of the page.

1. Diddy not wearing goggles.
2. Lulu's lilo doesn't have a pattern.
3. A chair is missing.
4. The shower is not working.
5. Polly has lost an earring.
6. The clown doesn't have a nose.

DASHING THROUGH THE SNOW

It was Christmas Eve night. Polly and her friends were getting ready for the midnight Christmas church service, but Polly was rather worried about the weather. Snow had been falling heavily all day and when the time came to set off, it was really deep!

They set out walking but the snow was much deeper than they had realised. Soon Fifi and Pixie were feeling tired and even Diddy's strong legs were aching!

'We must stop for a rest!' exclaimed Pixie, puffing and panting.

'I can't take my car out in the snow,' Polly told Diddy and Wee Willie. 'It's much too deep and dangerous to drive.'

'Don't worry, Polly,' said Lulu. 'We can walk to the church. It won't take long and it will be fun!'

Polly looked at her watch. It would soon be midnight and they would never make it to the church in time for the beginning of the service!

'Polly,' said Diddy, 'I've thought of something! You come

with me, the others can wait here.'

Polly wondered what Diddy was up to, but she asked her friends to wait and went with him. They didn't go far, only to the stables on Polly's farm.

'Why have you brought me here, Diddy?' asked Polly, mystified. She soon found out! Diddy opened the stable door and called softly to Polly's ponies, Frosty and Misty. The ponies trotted out into the cold night air.

'Put their coats on, Polly!' hurried Diddy. 'Next we're calling on my friend Jack at the farmhouse.'

Meanwhile, Lulu, Pixie and Wee Willie were stamping their feet to keep warm. Fifi was wishing she'd stayed indoors with a nice

cup of hot chocolate!

Suddenly, they saw Polly and Diddy coming towards them riding on a farm trailer pulled by Frosty and Misty!

'Wow!' gasped Wee Willie.

'It's the fastest trailer in Tiny World! Hurrah for Frosty and Misty! Hurrah for Polly and Diddy!'

'Quick!' shouted Polly. 'Jump in! We should just make it in time for the midnight service!'

Everyone scrambled on board the trailer and the two ponies trotted happily along the snowy streets to the church. It looked beautiful, lit up with Christmas lights and with a huge decorated fir tree outside.

As her friends filed through the church doors into the warmth, Polly paused to give her two ponies a big hug.

'I bet you'll get an extra bag of apples each from Father Christmas,' she told them. 'Thank you Frosty and Misty!'

Copy Colour Clock

Can you tell the time? It's easy with the Funtime Clock! See if you can copy the clock, square by square, into the empty grid. Then you can colour it too!

The Haunted Ballet

Tina searched her dressing room in the Grand Ballet Theatre. She and Rosie were rehearsing their roles in the "Babes in the Wood" ballet, but Tina had lost her ballet shoes and she couldn't dance without them!

Rosie came in without knocking. She looked cross!

'Tina!' she scolded. 'I've been waiting for you on stage for ages! The orchestra is ready to play for us! You know the rehearsal starts at two o'clock, so why are you not on stage like everyone else?'

Tina blushed. This was the third time this week and she knew Rosie was getting fed up with her.

'I've lost my ballet shoes again,' she muttered.

'Oh, for goodness sake, Tina!' grumbled Rosie. 'Again? I've never met anyone who loses things as much as you! You can borrow my spare shoes… just come on!'

But when Tina and Rosie arrived on the stage, there, right

in the middle of the spotlight, were Tina's missing ballet shoes!

Tina snatched them up. 'Someone's been dancing in these!' she announced. 'They're still warm! It's not funny, whoever did it!' She looked around at the company of dancers, but nobody admitted to having taken her shoes.

After rehearsal, Rosie went to her dressing room to change. As she sat in front of the mirror combing her long hair, she saw a girl's pale face appear in the glass for a few seconds, then fade away.

Rosie spun around in her seat, but there was no-one in the room with her.

'Who's there?' she called. 'Who's playing tricks?'

But no-one answered.

In the week leading up to the opening of the show, other strange things happened in the theatre. The orchestra's music sheets were changed around, so the violinist found himself playing the part of the trumpet and the kettle drummer had the notes for the harp!

Tina's shoes disappeared and turned up again in the most unusual places, inside the horn of the tuba or in the ice cream seller's tray! And Rosie kept seeing a strange dark-haired girl with a pale face watching wistfully from the wings during rehearsals. When she came off the stage and tried to find the girl, there was never any sign of her! Rosie didn't know who she was but she was sure she had something to do with all the odd things that were happening.

One day, Polly was rummaging through the props box, looking for some ostrich feathers to sew into Rosie's costume. She found a newspaper clipping that was one hundred years old! Everyone gathered round to listen as she read it out. It was about a ballet

that had been performed in the theatre over a hundred years ago and it showed a picture of the girl who'd danced the lead role!

'May I see?' asked Rosie, taking the flimsy paper and looking at the picture. It was the girl she kept seeing in the theatre! Rosie's eyes opened wide, but she decided not to tell the others. No-one else had

ever mentioned seeing the girl. 'Maybe she's a g-ghost!' thought Rosie, with a little shiver.

At last, the morning of the show arrived. The theatre was a bustle of noise and activity. The dancers were doing their last-minute practice, when suddenly Tina fell over and hurt her ankle.

'Quickly, get the doctor!' said Polly, as she and Midge carried Tina backstage into her dressing room. As Rosie ran behind them, someone caught her arm. It was the girl from the picture! Rosie just stared at her.

'I am Anna! Please, let me dance!' the girl begged. 'I knew you would need me! You understand, don't you? Please?' Then she disappeared behind the curtains.

The doctor was with Tina when Rosie arrived at her dressing room.

'No dancing for you, young lady!' he announced. 'That's a nasty sprain you have there!'

Everyone felt very sorry for Tina, but what were they going to do about the show? Rosie gulped and spoke up.

'I know someone who could dance Tina's part…' she said.

'Thank heavens for that!' said the choreographer. 'Now, I think we should get Tina settled where she can watch the show and then we really must get on! Come

along, please!'

As the curtain rose on the performance, Rosie felt very nervous. Suppose Anna didn't show up? What if she were a terrible dancer? But she needn't have worried! Anna glided across the stage like an angel! The show was a huge success!

When they took their final curtain call, with the audience clapping and cheering like mad, Rosie stood next to Anna in the line up. Anna held her hand and squeezed it very tightly.

'Thank you, Rosie,' she whispered, in her funny soft voice. 'Tina will be well enough to dance the show next time so I must go now, but thank you so much.'

They bowed again, and when Rosie looked back, Anna was gone. 'Goodbye, Anna,' she whispered. 'Thank you for your brilliant dancing!'

Tina was soon better and able to dance her role again. But Rosie never forgot her first "Babes in the Wood" partner, Anna the ghostly ballerina.

TINY WORLD™
1
2
3
4
5
6
7
8
9
10
Can you work out which of the drawings below match to the places shown in this photograph of Tiny World?
A
B
C
D
E
F
G
H
I
J
Village Church 1,G Village School 2,C
Pizza Place 3,A Country House 4,B
Cosy Cottage 5,D Ski Chalet 6,H
Toy Shop 7,I Pet Shop 8,E
Holiday Cottage 9,F Beach Cafe 10,J

Polly Pocket®
TINY WORLD
TOUR
Late for school!
THROW 6 TO MOVE AGAIN.
12
13
10
9
8
TOYS
PETS
Play with kittens in Pet Shop.
HAVE ANOTHER TURN.
15
16
17
Whoosh down To
Shop slide!
MOVE ON 3 SPACE
Sunbathe at Holiday
Cottage.
MISS A TURN.
6
5
4
2
19
20
START
Pick flowers in Cosy Cottage garden.
MISS A TURN.
MILK
BEACH CLUB
Here's a great game you can play with your friends. You'll need a dice and a shaker and some different coloured counters or buttons. Place the counters on Start and move round the board the number of spaces shown on the dice. If you land on a space with a picture, you must do what the message says. The first person to reach the Pizza Place is the winner.
Have fun!

Diddy's Disco
32
33
31
Snowball fight at Ski Chalet!
GO BACK 3 SPACES.
35
36
29
28
Dance the night away at Country House disco.
THROW 1 TO MOVE AGAIN.
27
Watch wedding at Village Church.
HAVE ANOTHER TURN.
38
26
PIZZA
QUEUE HERE
CAFE
23
24
25
Big queue at Pizza Place!
MISS A TURN WHILE WAITING.
FINISH
Go for swim at Beach Cafe.
MOVE ON 3 SPACES.
FINISH off a Pizza!
Well done!

Polly and Midge were flying out on a fact-finding mission to China! Midge had explained to Polly that the Giant Panda, which lived in China, was an endangered species.

'What do you mean, Midge?' asked Polly. 'What is an endangered species?'

'It means that there are not very many giant pandas left in the world,' said Midge. 'And they need our help if they are to survive. Otherwise they could easily become extinct!'

'Extinct?' gasped Polly. 'You mean like the dinosaurs? There wouldn't be any left at all?'

'That's right,' nodded Midge.

'So you can see how important it is that we try to help them survive, can't you? There weren't any people around to help in the dinosaurs' time.'

'The dinosaurs would probably have eaten them, if people had been around though, wouldn't they?' Polly asked.

'Don't be daft Polly,' grinned Midge. 'Dinosaurs were mainly vegetarians! Look, we're landing!'

The girls took a rickshaw taxi to their hotel. After dinner, Midge telephoned the people who had invited them to China.

'The headman of the village is going to take us to see some giant pandas tomorrow,' she told Polly. 'Isn't it exciting?'

Next morning the headman took them on horseback into the mountains. It was a long way, but it was worth it when he showed them where a panda and her cub were feeding on bamboo shoots.

'Oh, aren't they beautiful?' gasped Polly. 'We must make sure

they don't become extinct! Wouldn't it be better to keep them in a zoo Midge?'

'No way Polly!' snorted Midge crossly. 'How would you like to spend your life living in a cage, instead of being free to live in the mountains?'

Polly thought about it. 'You're right Midge,' she said. 'It can't be much fun to be a prisioner all your life! Let's ask the headman how we can help!'

The girls didn't know it, but the headman's English wasn't very good. And Midge and Polly didn't speak any Chinese at all! But somehow they managed to explain that they would like to learn how to take care of the pandas.

The headman told them that he had to come to the mountains

every day, to make sure that there were plenty of bamboo shoots for the pandas and to check that no big stones had fallen into the river, damming it and drying it up.

'Also make sure no bears or tigers frighten pandas,' he continued, counting on his fingers. 'You still want to help?'

The girls nodded their heads

quickly. 'Of course!'

'Then you come every day to mountains for time of your holiday!' he said. 'When holiday over, you come see me again!' The girls agreed.

Back at their hotel, Polly was thinking about what the headman had said. She suddenly realised that the headman thought they had offered to look after the mountain pandas for three whole weeks!

'But that's not what we wanted to do at all!' gasped Midge. 'We want to know how we can prevent them from becoming extinct!'

'They won't become extinct for the next three weeks anyway,' groaned Polly. 'We'll have to go and check on them every day... we promised!'

And they did exactly that! Every morning, they saddled up their horses and rode into the mountains. They made sure that the pandas had enough to eat and once they had to chase away a nasty looking snake. When the river turned to a trickle, they rode upstream and cleared away a big pile of rocks that had fallen into the water, damming the flow. At the end of three weeks they were exhausted, but pleased with their hard work.

'And at least we didn't see any tigers or bears,' Midge remarked on their last morning in China.

'Thank goodness!' said Polly. 'We'd better hurry Midge, we still have to go and say goodbye to the headman before our plane leaves!'

The headman was waiting for them. He smiled and handed them each a small package.

'You have done good work,' he said in his sing-song voice. 'You have learned much about giant panda. Now you can tell others.'

And he bowed low, his long beard touching the ground, before shaking hands and saying goodbye.

On the plane, the girls were silent, thinking how much they would miss the pandas and the beautiful mountains. Midge remembered the packages the headman had given them.

'I wonder what they are?' she said, opening hers. Inside was a baby panda furry toy!

Polly laughed and opened her package. It was another panda. 'Aren't they lovely, Midge?' she said. 'And a lot easier to look after than real ones!'

PIZZA PLACE PUZZLE
Polly's Pizza Place is always full of hungry customers ready for a delicious pizza! But today there are some very strange things happening! Look carefully at the picture and see how many odd things you can spot. Then see how many tiny mice are hiding in the picture, waiting for some cheese.
Pizza
Answers: Polly's dressed for diving! The chef is a pig! Two pandas are smoochy-dancing! Two clowns are juggling! A rhino's reading a newspaper! The parrot's a banana! Diddy's skateboarding on the ceiling! There are 5 tiny mice hiding.

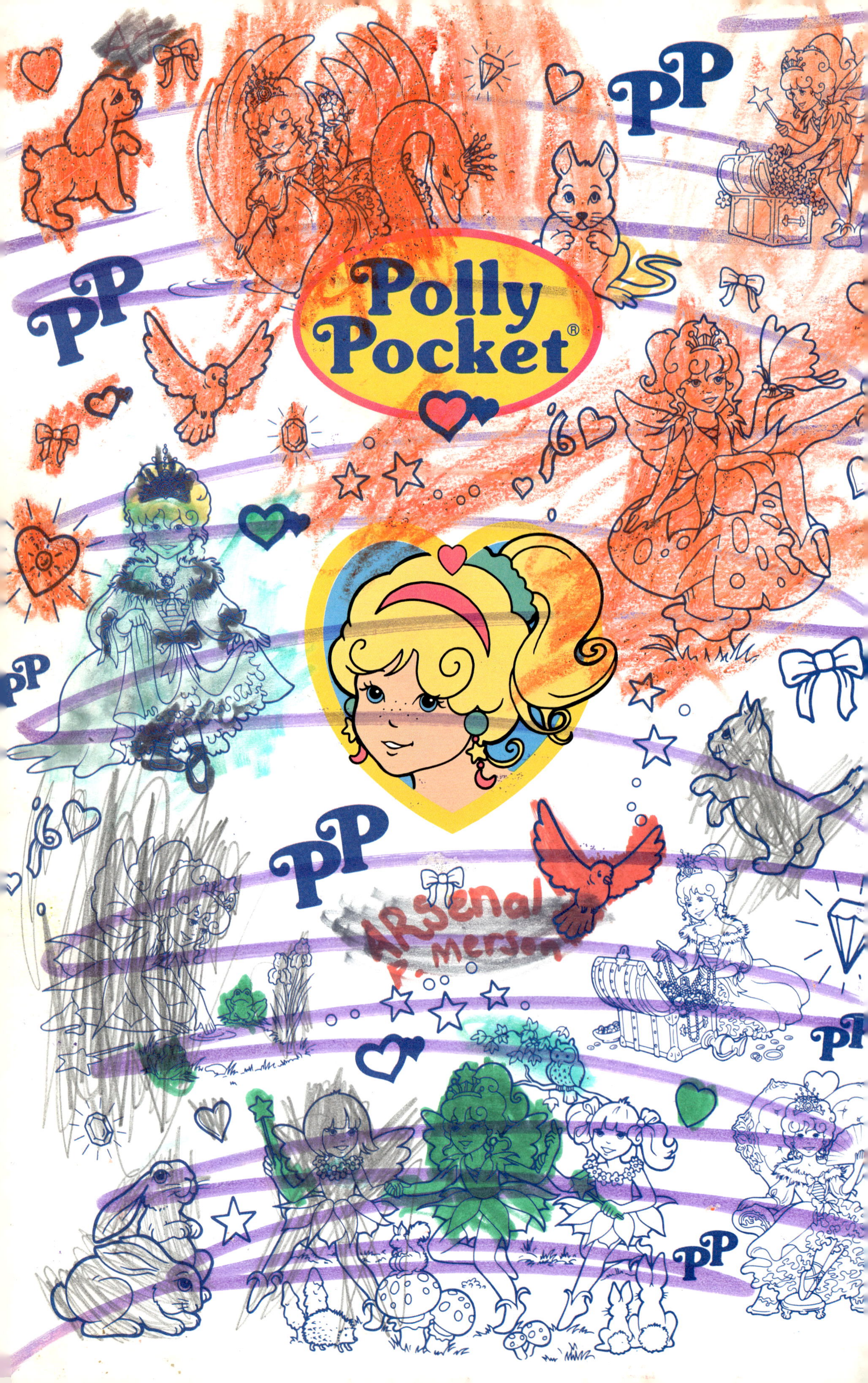
Polly Pocket®